# Bali

## ISLE OF LIGHT

# Bali

## ISLE OF LIGHT

Text by

**Tan Chung Lee**

**Marshall Cavendish**
Editions

**Photo Credits**

Jill Gocher: Cover, 1, 8–9, 10, 12 (top left & right), 14 (top & bottom left), 15, 18, 25, 51, 66, 72, 73, 74 (bottom left), 75, 81, 86, 87, 88–89, 91, 92, 128; Hutchison Library: 12 (bottom right), 27 (top), 54 (right), 55, 56, 58 (top left), 62, 64, 65 (left), 67 (bottom), 68, 78 (bottom), 90, 93, 100–101, 105, 108–109, 115, 118 (bottom left), 119, 121 (bottom), 122, 136–137; Bes Stock: 4–5, 16–17, 24, 26, 28, 29 (top & bottom right), 60 (top), 61 (right), 63 (top), 67 (top), 69 (top), 79, 107 (top), 113 (top left), 114 (bottom left), 117 (top), 118 (top & bottom right), 129; International Photobank, UK: 14 (bottom right), 27 (bottom left), 53, 58 (top right & bottom left), 78 (top), 84–85, 94 (bottom left & right), 99, 116; Renata Holzbachova/ Philippe Benet: 2, 27, (bottom right), 33 (top left), 52 (bottom), 94 (top left), 104, 140, 141, 144; Focus Team—Italy: 11, 63 (bottom left), 69 (bottom left), 82, 83, 98, 102, 110, 123; Christine Osborne Pictures: 12 (bottom left), 29 (bottom left), 54 (left), 57, 61 (left), 80, 94 (top right), 107 (bottom), 113 (bottom right); Haga Library, Japan: 60 (bottom), 65 (right), 76–77, 96–97, 117 (bottom left & right); Christopher Wee: 7, 23, 134–135; Wendy Chan: 52 (top left), 58 (bottom right), 103, 106; HBL Network: 30–31, 113 (top right & bottom left); Tan Chung Lee: 34, 36, 37, 38, 39 40, 41, 46, 47, 124, 125, 126, 127; Carl-Bernd Kaehlig: 19; Richard I'Anson: 95; Hans Hayden: 13, 42, 43, 44, 45, 48–49, 50, 52 (top right), 74 (bottom right), 75 (bottom right), 114 (bottom right); Mark De Fraeye: 112

**Copyright © 2005 Marshall Cavendish International (Asia) Private Limited**

Published by Marshall Cavendish Editions
An imprint of Marshall Cavendish International
1 New Industrial Road, Singapore 536196

Other Marshall Cavendish Offices

Marshall Cavendish Ltd. 119 Wardour Street, London W1F OUW, UK • Marshall Cavendish Corporation. 99 White Plains Road, Tarrytown NY 10591-9001, USA • Marshall Cavendish Beijing. D31A, Huatingjiayuan, No. 6, Beisihuanzhonglu, Chaoyang District, Beijing, The People's Republic of China, 100029 • Marshall Cavendish International (Thailand) Co Ltd. 253 Asoke, 12th Flr, Sukhumvit 21 Road, Klongtoey Nua, Wattana, Bangkok 10110, Thailand • Marshall Cavendish (Malaysia) Sdn Bhd, Times Subang, Lot 46, Subang Hi-Tech Industrial Park, Batu Tiga, 40000 Shah Alam, Selangor Darul Ehsan, Malaysia

Marshall Cavendish is a trademark of Times Publishing Limited

**National Library Board Singapore Cataloguing in Publication Data**
Tan, Chung Lee, 1949-
Bali : isle of light / Tan Chung Lee. – Singapore :
Marshall Cavendish Editions, 2005. p. cm.
ISBN : 981-261-076-6
Bali Island (Indonesia) – Description and travel.  2. Bali Island
(Indonesia) – Social life and customs.  3. Bali Island (Indonesia) – Pictorial works.  I. Title.
DS647.B2
959.86 -- dc21            SLS2005035037

Printed in Singapore by Utopia Printers Pte Ltd

# CONTENTS

# INTRODUCTION

Bali... Its very name evokes images of an exotic land, created by spectacular scenes of terraced rice fields and moody volcanoes, cobalt-blue seas, dancers in resplendent costumes and lissom native beauties.

Since early times, Bali has enchanted those who have come to know it, from Dutch explorers and European artists to today's peripatetic tourist. It is astonishing that the island, among one of Indonesia's smallest, could figure so largely on the world map and that its fame has reached the farthest points of the globe.

Bali, when you come to think of it, is a bit of an aberration; its 3.2 million people are mostly Hindu (95 per cent) while 88 per cent of Indonesia's population of 238.5 million are Muslims. Yet, it is this difference that has given the island its special charm, for it has bestowed upon its people a unique culture that dictates life's daily tempo. It is this same Bali-Hindu animistic religion that has helped shape the Balinese character, temperament and outlook, and enabled them to cope with the many intrusions of the outside world. It is the reason why, despite the onslaught of foreign influences wrought by mass tourism, despite the changes that have inevitably taken over its urban areas, Bali is still rural at heart and its people at ease with their place in the world.

A relief map of Bali reveals an onion paper surface running across the island from west to east. This represents a volcanic chain of mountains that is the geological continuation of Java's peaks. Only the tapered southern end of the island is not mountainous. It is here, on the foothills of mountains and in the valleys, and along the coast, that Bali's people have settled into cities, towns and villages. How Bali and its people came about is a story rooted as much in historical facts and geological data as it is in magic and legends.

*A temple in Mengwi (above) and a young dancer (facing page) are two aspects of Bali's unique culture which centres largely on religion and the arts.*

*Temple festivals involve the participation of young and old alike. The temple grounds and its stone guardians are decorated, the latter draped with a checked black-and-white cloth said to ward off evil or brightened with flowers. Offerings of food and flowers are brought in for the gods (facing page).*

*Left: The temples of Bali are unmistakeable, with multi-tiered thatched roofs that are seven, nine or 11 in number, depending on the deity to which it is dedicated. The 11-tiered temple, such as this one in Tuban, was built in honour of Siva the Destroyer, the greatest of the Hindu gods. A nine-tiered temple represents Vishnu the Preserver while a seven-tiered temple is a tribute to Brahma the Creator.*

13

*The Lotus Café in Ubud (right) was one of the first of many trendy cafés that continue to mushroom in Bali. Facing page: Bali's landscape is dominated by lush terraced rice fields such as these.
Below: The Balinese are skilled artisans, turning out carvings in different styles. Originally, they started by sculpting for the gods, honing their skills as they created religious objects.
Following pages: Outrigger canoes and pleasure boats on Lake Bratan await customers.*

# BIRTH OF BALI

Long before the continental land drift, Bali was enjoined with what is now Java, Sumatra and Malaysia. Then, when the landmasses split, Bali also became divided from Java by a three-kilometre strait. Geologically, Bali is thus a continuation of Java, as evidenced by peaks such as Gunung Batukau (2,315 metres), Abang (2,152 metres), Batur (1,700 metres) and Agung (the highest at 3,142 metres), which are part of the Javanese chain of mountains.

Legend, however, gives a different twist to how Bali was born.

A long time ago, there was a king of Java whose son incurred his displeasure. Deciding to banish him from the kingdom, the monarch brought his son to the narrowest section of the island—an isthmus that connected the larger part of Java to a peninsula-shaped tip. He told his son to leave. As soon as he lost sight of the boy on the horizon, the king marked out a line across the sands of the isthmus with his finger to separate their two worlds. This very line is where the waters of the Java Sea and Indian Ocean meet, clearly dividing Java from Bali—the peninsula that was lopped off and became an island.

Science, of course, tells us a different story. Bali is located on the volatile Pacific Belt's Ring of Fire and its birth, like that of so many volcanic islands, was characteristically cataclysmic.

Eons ago, as far back as 100,000 years, hot magma rising from the sea spewed lava, gases and other materials on the surface that later settled down to become mountain peaks. Bursts of explosions alternating with periods of cooling down resulted in the formation of island masses, one of which was known, since the 6th century, as Po'li. It was described by a travelling missionary from China as a place of luxuriant vegetation, and ruled by a Hindu kingdom. That Po'li is believed to be Bali today.

*Sunrise over the northern coast of Bali (above), an island where man and nature have harmonised so perfectly that it moved India's first Prime Minister, Jawaharlal Nehru, to call it 'The Dawn of the World'.*
*Facing page: Carved out of a cliffside of Gunung Kawi, near Tampaksiring, are ancient royal tombs said to date back to the 11th century.*

# Early History

Bali is believed to have been inhabited as far back as the Bronze Age by groups of proto-Malays, who had settled there along the migration route from South China to the South Seas. Although passing sailors from China were said to have contributed ideas that helped in the civilisation of a primitive Bali over the centuries, the greatest influences came from India, spread by traders and passing travellers who laid the foundations of Balinese language and art, and its socio-political institutions. Part of the influence also emanated from neighbouring Java, which was the centre of the Hindu-Javanese Majapahit Empire, from 1294 to 1527.

At the zenith of its glory in the 14th century, the Majapahit Empire ruled the seas from India to China. It was around the mid-14th century that Bali was brought firmly under its wing during the reign of Hayam Wuruk. It also marked the period when elements of Hinduism began to infuse Bali's fine arts, architecture, sculpture and dance forms.

However, in the 16th century, Majapahit lost its control of the regional maritime trade to an ascending Islamic power that had its base in Malacca, and the death of Hayam Wuruk finally led to a distintegration of the empire. The collapse of Majapahit was accompanied by an exodus of Hindus who felt they could not carry on in a Muslim Java. They fled to Bali, which was already Hinduised and conveniently close by.

The result of this migration was an enrichment of Balinese culture as the new ideas brought in by the refugees, who came from all levels of society—from priests and artists to soldiers and artisans—were meshed with the existing way of life.

*Pictures of the royal family still decorate the palace walls of Karangasem (below left). A portrait of the Raja of Buleleng (which came under Balinese rule in 1882) and his family (below). Dutch officials (facing page) in Gianyar.*

## The Arrival of the Dutch

The 16th century, too, marked the first contacts Bali had with the Dutch. Cornelius de Houtman, who led the initial expedition on behalf of the Dutch East India Company in 1597, wrote about the island's beauty and wealth. His superiors, however, were more pre-occupied with establishing control over Java and Indonesia's spice islands and left Bali alone for the next 200 years.

In the 1800s, there was renewed contact be-tween the Balinese and the Dutch but they were less auspicious as they finally resulted in six Dutch military expeditions against Bali.

It all began in 1839 when a Dutch trader, Mads Lange, opened a trading post in Kuta which developed into an important supply station and port of call for passing ships.

Trouble started when a number of shipwrecks occurred and the Balinese looted the vessels believing it was their divine right to do so since the ships had run aground on their shores. Lange tried to mediate but to no avail. The Dutch launched the first of their military offensives during which both sides suffered losses and increased their resentment against each other.

Matters came to a head in 1906 when a Chi-nese-owned vessel floundered on a reef in Sanur and was looted by inhabitants in the area. The Dutch demanded that the Raja of Badung pay the compensation sought by the Chinese. The raja refused and he was supported by the rajas of neighbouring kingdoms.

The Dutch mounted yet another expedition, their sixth, to force the raja to submit. As Dutch troops marched towards the raja's palace in Badung, the raja, realising the hopelessness of the situation, went with his followers to meet the Dutch and committed *puputan* (mass ritual suicide, where one walks straight into enemy fire with fake guns drawn).

This incident, known as Puputan Badung, was followed by other *puputan* led by other rajas, and even the Dewa Agung of the kingdom of Klungkung. By 1908, the Dutch came to rule all of Bali.

## Modern History

The Second World War and the brief occupation of Indonesia by the Japanese had little impact on Bali. On August 17, 1950, when Indonesia's nationalists won their struggle of independence against the Dutch, Bali was incorporated into the new republic as one of its provinces.

However, another blight on Bali's history occurred on September 30, 1965 when an uprising, believed to have been staged by the Communist Party of Indonesia (PKI), led to the killing of thousands of Balinese who were believed to have been Communist sympathisers. The blood-bath eventually caused the banning of the PKI and the forced retirement of the then ruling president,

Sukarno, who handed over emergency powers to General Suharto. The latter became president in March 1967 and ruled, with an iron fist, for more than 32 years.

Growing opposition against Suharto in the later years of his rule culminated in protests and riots. His downfall in 1998 led to the appointment of B.J. Habibie as interim president. In 1999, Abdurrahman Wahid became president but widespread unrest continued, especially when the latter became embroiled in corruption scandals. Finally, on August 23, 2000, Wahid was dismissed as president by Parliament. Vice-President Megawati Sukarnoputri, Sukarno's eldest daughter, and one of Bali's favourite scions, (she was born there), was appointed to replace Wahid.

Following an unremarkable period of rule, Megawati stepped down as president in September 2004, having lost out to former general Susilo Bambang Yudhoyono in Indonesia's first-ever direct presidential elections.

The Puputan Memorial commemorates the puputan on September 20, 1906 when the Raja of Badung (now Denpasar) and his entourage committed mass suicide rather than submit to the Dutch.

# THE URBAN LANDSCAPE

**D**espite intense tourism development in Bali, holidaymakers can always find quiet places of repose. The sitting room of a duplex cottage of a typical resort hotel (above) and a beachside cottage on Lovinia Beach (facing page).

In the very popular restaurant-café of Made's Warung in Kuta are some black-and-white photographs showing Kuta as it was in 1972. There was no road then, just a path that led past foliage—the odd *warung* (food-stall) and restaurant on either side of it—to the deserted golden palm-fringed beach of Kuta at the end of it. Another photograph shows a young Balinese girl in a resplendent costume carrying offerings piled high upon her head.

The two images of an idyllic Bali that seduced so many artists, photographers and other visitors in the past have met two distinct fates. The first scene has vanished—forever. Today, Kuta Beach is right next to a main road lined with restaurants, cafés, jeep and motorcycle rental agencies, fashion stores and souvenir shops. The road is choked with traffic and there is a constant din from blaring horns. Kuta Beach itself is no longer an unspoilt haven. Jostling for space are sunbathers, surfers, vendors and women offering beach massages. The second image is quintessential Bali and you can still find it today. Wherever you may be, you will often encounter colourful lines of young girls and women, demurely walking, Indian file, to the nearest temple with offerings on their heads.

The first tourists to Bali were said to have arrived in the 1930s but the biggest inflow of visitors from the outside world began in the 1970s when a wave of mass tourism, prompted by cheap air travel and a shrinking world, brought foreigners to the island's shores. The legendary beauty of Bali and its people had spread far and wide for it had already been well-documented in many books and people were curious to come see it for themselves.

All this spawned a thriving tourist industry; hotels went up to cater to the burgeoning arrivals and in the words of a representative of the Indonesian Tourism Promotion Board, "Bali has been selling itself ever since".

# Transformation

With the influx of tourists, the face of Bali began to change, at least, the southern 'urban' area. In the 1970s, Denpasar, the capital, was still a sleepy, dusty town with a few streets. The traditional village of Sanur, transformed into an enclave by foreign residents, was Bali's first tourist resort with a handful of upmarket hotels catering to a moneyed clientele. The fishing village of Kuta with its *losmens* (family-run lodgings) was a haven for the less well-heeled traveller and Australian surfers who were drawn by news of an unspoilt beach with great surf and spectacular sunsets.

Today, Denpasar is a bustling city of some 400,000 people. It is now a concrete jungle of shops, restaurants, office complexes and traffic-snarled streets. It has spilled beyond its original boundaries, gobbling up neighbouring villages and rice fields along the way, and blurring the lines that had previously divided it from Sanur and Kuta. Lately, Denpasar has pushed its boundaries northwards, and away from the crowded city centre, its landscape is surprisingly green and uncluttered, with only a scattering of houses.

The once elegant Sanur, too, has burgeoned. Crowded with luxury hotels, its previously quiet sidewalks are now lined with souvenir shops blaring loud music. Over-crowded Kuta is no longer the domain of the budget traveller. Upmarket hotels, trendy restaurants and fashion boutiques have given Kuta a touch of class. Kuta itself has spilled into Legian and Seminyak in the north, a now much preferred choice for those who prefer a more tranquil beach location.

The biggest impact of tourism is in the physical transformation of the urban landscape. Where Mas and Ubud were once truly villages with clusters of artists' studios, its roads soon became lined with shop after souvenir shop, studio after artist's studio—all selling, more or less, the same range of goods. But the impact has had some salutary effects as it created new avenues of employment and a boom economy, lessening the dependence on agriculture. What's more, the ever-adaptable Balinese have learnt to keep up with the times and changing tastes. For instance, these days, besides the usual traditional fare in its handicrafts and art, the Balinese offer ultra-modern,

*Poolside scenes at the Nusa Dua Beach Hotel (facing page and below right), Amandari (left) and the Segara Village Hotel (below, left) sum up the pleasures of Bali's resort life.*

'Zen'-influenced pieces to meet the demand for more contemporary styles.

Yet, as paradoxical as it may seem, despite the changes, much of Bali remains the same. The deeply spiritual Balinese have retained their cultural and religious rituals that they practise to keep harmony in their lives.

What's more, along the coast and deep in the heart of Bali, in the rural villages, as the visitor will discover, the rhythm of life beats as it always has, dictated by the weather, the planting seasons and the gods.

*The seaside delights of Bali are also well known. They include white sand beaches, massages while you sun bask, shopping from passing vendors and watersports for the more energetic.*
*Following pages: Surf's up! It was the discovery of Kuta's fabulous surf that brought surfseekers—and later the tourist hordes—to Bali's shores.*

29

*D*enpasar, once a sleepy town, has burgeoned to gobble up adjacent areas such as Kuta, which itself encroaches upon neighbouring Legian (facing page, top right). Facing page, bottom: Birdcages galore in Denpasar's market. Despite changes, the urban Balinese is still close to nature and is an avid bird enthusiast.

*T*extile shops, art galleries, handicraft stores, restaurants and cafés are symbols of Bali's urban landscape (right, below and facing page). Textiles vary from exquisite ikat cloths to colourful cotton prints while handicrafts include cast-iron objects, soapstone carvings, recycled stationery and papercraft, baskets and decorative pieces of carved furniture. For art, you can choose from traditional Balinese-style paintings to more modern abstract pieces. Many stores offer highly stylish and contemporary decorative accessories that would do any home-owner proud.

**K**uta was, for a long time, a tourist enclave boasting luxury hotels and a lively entertainment scene, a far cry from its early days as a simple fishing village. Its trendy restaurants and discos were a magnet for tourists. However, they became the target of Islamic extremists who, perceiving Kuta as a den of sin, set off two bombs in the town on October 12, 2002. Kuta and the rest of Bali suffered a sharp decline in tourism but just a few years later, the tourists have started to return. Slowly, Kuta is regaining its reputation as the entertainment hub of Bali (above and following page).

Despite being steeped in tradition, Bali displays a modern outlook.
Bottom, left: The re-invention of Kuta: many of its traditional shopfronts have given way to modern, all-glass stores, like this one, selling the latest in surfing gear, swimwear and sports attire.
Bottom, right: A jazz club in Ubud.
Left: Night entertainment still throbs in Bali.

# TROUBLE IN PARADISE

For a long time, Bali was the epitome of an idyllic tropical paradise. Even when other parts of Indonesia was racked by, mostly, sectarian conflicts and ethnic violence during the period of political unrest between 1999 and 2001, Bali was a veritable oasis of calm.

Life on the island was languid, and with homogeneity in the overwhelming Hindu population, ethnic conflicts were unthinkable. While tourists were advised by their governments to avoid other troubled parts of Indonesia, Bali was thriving. The island seemed 'untouchable' by all the goings-on elsewhere. It was a haven—a notion reinforced in 2000 when riots in neighbouring Lombok forced tourists, and locals alike, to flee to Bali to seek refuge.

Then, the improbable happened. Saturday, October 12, 2002 was like any other Saturday night in Kuta with tourists partying in its pubs, nightclubs and bars. It was in two of these venues—Paddy's Bar and the Sari Club—that two huge successive bomb explosions went off, around midnight, sparking off fires and creating total mayhem.

The attacks, said to have been the work of Islamic extremists with links to the Al-Qaeda movement, exacted a heavy toll. There was a loss of 203 lives, mostly tourists, and thousands more were injured. A sharp drop in tourist arrivals followed in the aftermath, hurting the tourism-dependent Balinese economy as shops and restaurants closed for business, hotels cut back on staff, and airlines curtailed their operations.

*Facing page: The Bali Peace Park marks the location of the Sari Club, which was one of the scenes of the terrorist attack in Kuta. The other was Paddy's Bar (above), now an empty piece of land.*

# The Aftermath and Recovery

As tourists started to return to Bali three years later, the economy began to recover. Those found responsible for the bombing were meanwhile sentenced to jail terms.

As terrible as the bombings were, some among the Balinese wonder whether it had been brought about by themselves, the result of 'karma'.

For some time, there had been concerns among the more conservative Balinese over how Kuta had been developing, willy-nilly, without any form of control, and how it was fast turning into a hedonistic enclave, far removed from the Balinese way of life. As it has often been remarked, "Kuta is not Bali at all."

The attacks led to much soul-searching and forced the Balinese to step back and re-examine the effects of overdevelopment and tourism. It prompted a re-look into how they could restore harmony in their lives and create a balance between the need to develop and the need to ensure minimal impact on local culture and the environment. Greater scrutiny has since been given to the building of new resorts, for example, to avoid damage to the environment.

However, despite the self-doubts in the aftermath of the bombing, Kuta has still not shed its 'fun' image, though this is now somewhat subdued. Many of the traditional shopfronts in town have recently been transformed into modern, all-glass buildings housing surf gear and the latest in sporting wear, exported mainly from Australia. Kuta also boasts a new ultra-modern shopping complex and a discotheque built in a striking contemporary design that stands out at night with its Greek-style columns bathed in lights.

*The Bali memorial in Kuta, dedicated to those who lost their lives in the terrorist attack on October 12, 2002, stands close to the spot where the bombings occurred (left and below). Like a mural on a wall, the names of the victims of the Bali bombing and their nationalities are etched in marble as part of the Bali memorial (facing page).*

Perhaps, there was a need for Kuta to show the world that it is business as usual in its own little slice of tropical paradise. Indeed, its annual week-long Kuta Karnival in June, inaugurated in 2003 as 'A Celebration of Life', is just that—a means of showing that tourism is still alive and well in Bali. The carnival, centred around Kuta beach, features seven days of music, a street parade, beach games and water sports competitions, fashion shows and a food festival.

Nor has Kuta forgotten the day when paradise was lost. In deference to those killed in the bombings, an open-air candle-lit memorial service is held every year on October 12 at the sites of the attacks.

## The Bali Memorial

Erected to remember the dead from the Bali bombing of 2002, the Bali Memorial is now one of the most visited sites in Kuta. The memorial names all the countries and victims of the attacks. It stands next to an empty plot of land where Paddy's Bar once stood and facing the 'Bali Peace Park', the site of the former Sari Club. The ever-spiritual Balinese have decided to leave this site untouched so as not to disturb the souls of the dead.

Marking its comeback to Kuta is the new Paddy's Bar, a stone's throw from its former site, which was one of the scenes of the terrorist attack of October 12, 2002.

# SPA CULTURE

S pas may have been a 'Western' phenomenon, born out of the age-old European healing tradition of 'taking the waters'. This was achieved by either inhaling the health-giving waters, imbibing them, bathing in them or inhaling its vapours.

However, unlike the European spas, which use the mineral-rich waters of natural springs to cure ailments, the tropical spa is more about body treatments, beauty and wellness.

As a tropical spa destination, Bali reigns supreme.

There may not be any natural springs available but what its tropical spas offer are a refuge for the stressed, a place where one can relax amid much greenery and natural surroundings and be treated with traditional Balinese massage and healing therapies, using local herbs and spices.

It is no exaggeration to say that Bali probably started the wave of tropical spas that has swept much of Asia in recent years.

This combination of the gentle Balinese spirit, age-old massage therapies and salubrious surroundings is one reason Bali will retain its charm, whatever the vicissitudes of tourism.

*Bali reigns supreme in the world of tropical spas. Resorts dotted around the island offer a myriad of body and beauty treatments in dedicated spa centres focused around swimming pools (top), some of which even boast water therapy massage jets. Entrance to Nusa Dua Resort's swimming pool and spa (left).*

Alfresco massages in outdoor pavilions add to the charm of this spa (right); the hydrotherapy pool of *The Grand Mirage Resort Bali* offers a variety of water jets that massage the body (bottom, left)—an alternative to the more traditional form of massage (bottom, right).

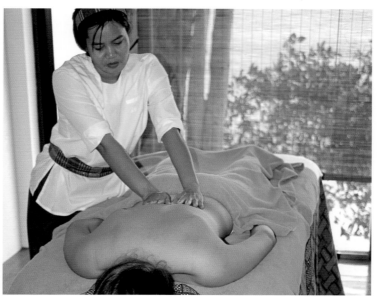

*A*n outdoor shower in a typical Balinese spa (left).

**A**s an example of the adaptability of the Balinese are the island's 'new-age' resorts, which demonstrate the artful combination of Balinese tradition and modern lifestyles. Every one of these resorts seems to be more modern and more 'Zen' in decor than the previous one. Built Balinese in style but with contemporary furnishings, they are set in spectacular scenery such as the Maya Ubud (facing page) and usually boasting swimming pools with infinity edges (left) and the ubiquitous spa. Following pages: A typical resort in Bali—exuding serenity.

# LIFE AMID THE RICE TERRACES

Hewn out of the fertile sides of Bali's volcanic mountains are steps climbing skywards. These are no ordinary steps but terraces built for the cultivation of *padi* or rice, a life-sustaining staple for the Balinese. So important is *padi* that every arable inch of land is devoted to its cultivation. The Balinese even have a rice goddess, Bhatari Sri, to protect the crop and you will see shrines dedicated to her dotting the rice terraces.

It is amid these spectacular emerald staircases to heaven that the majority of Balinese live, work and play. The rhythms of life are dictated by the sun, starting at the first break of light around 5 am and ending, equally early, by 6 pm, when darkness falls.

The day begins with a refreshing *mandi* (bath) in a running stream, from water diverted from a sluice or from a well. Then it's time to fetch water to the home for cooking and cleaning. The woman of the house sweeps the compound clean and prepares offerings of a few grains of rice, flowers and salt in small squares of banana leaves to placate evil spirits so that the day will proceed harmoniously. She places the offerings in front of her house, at the main gate and before the family shrine. Then it's off to the market to sell freshly harvested vegetables and fruit, or handwoven baskets or weavings, all carried on the head. In the meantime, the man of the house puts out his prized cages of fighting roosters to forage on the grass before heading off to work in the rice fields.

At midday, the family gathers for a simple lunch of rice, some fish, chicken or duck with chilli peppers on the side. The sun is blazing hot at this hour so the men take a rest before they return to the rice terraces in the cooler late afternoon. For the women, it's the chance to continue their weaving of baskets. When dusk falls, the men return from work. It's time for another *mandi* followed by dinner and a chat with neighbours or perhaps watching a village dance or theatrical performance.

*Bali would be a very different place without rice. Even young children are roped in to help in field chores. Although it is the men who work outdoors, it is not uncommon to see women toiling beside them, helping in planting, harvesting, threshing the husks and bringing home the sacks of grains.*

51

# Bali's Subak System

If Bali's rice terraces look very orderly, it's because they are well run. Indeed, since the 11th century, Balinese farmers have organised themselves into a sort of co-operative system known as the *subak*. Each *subak* looks after the *sawah* (rice fields) that are fed by the same waterway. The cooperative looks after the construction and maintenance of waterworks such as canals, aqueducts and sluices to ensure a regular distribution and supply of water to the fields, some of which may be far-flung. This wet-rice cultivation method enables two crops to be grown a year.

Apart from water distribution, the *subak* also organises the timetable for rice cultivation such as the sowing of seeds and the transplanting of seedlings. In the five-month period between sowing and harvesting, during which the seedlings are carefully looked after, the cooperative organises festivals and offerings at the *subak* temple and rituals in the fields dedicated to the rice goddess in the hope that she will ensure a favourable growing season.

All farmer-members of the *subak* are expected to join in the ceremonies. And of course, the members can reap the benefits of their cooperation, come harvest time, when the *subak* divides the spoils of ripened golden rice grains among them.

*Villagers hard at work preparing the rice fields for the transplanting of seedlings while ducks are brought in to feed on insects which can do harm to the young seedlings.*

*O*fferings are made to the shrine of the rice goddess, Bhatari Sri, so that she may ensure a bountiful harvest of golden sheafs of grains (above). Facing page: Many hands make light work. This is especially true of the subak which is unique to Bali. Farmers who are members of the subak get together to work on their land by sharing tasks such as irrigating the fields, planting rice and reaping the harvest, and distributing the spoils among them.

## The Village

Even more highly organised than the *subak* is the village to which everyone belongs from the moment of birth. The village is more than just a place where a family lives; it functions as a social, economic and religious unit.

The Balinese village enjoys an idyllic setting, amid lush rice fields and surrounded by fruit trees such as the rambutan, jackfruit, banana, papaya, mango and the ubiquitous coconut palm—all grown for the shade they provide, the fruits they yield and the wood for fuel.

Villages typically flank the sides of the main road with thatched-roof mud walls. They run in typical Balinese fashion, in a north-south direction, from the mountain to the sea. Behind the walls are the family units, each occupying an enclosed compound.

The hub of the village is the crossroads where you will find the social and religious gathering places. Among them are three important temples: the mountain-oriented *pura puseh* (temple of origin dedicated to ancestor worship); the central *pura desa* (village temple) for day-to-day ceremonies; and *pura dalem* (temple of the dead) facing the sea and located on the village outskirts near the cemetery, where the dead are temporarily buried before cremation.

A *bale agung* or meeting hall, next to which is an open space for the market, an ornately carved *kulkul* (bell tower), the *wantilan* or cock-fighting area and the *waringin* or sacred banyan tree complete the village set-up.

The village in Bali is a highly organised unit where people live, work, play and worship together. Villages typically flank the sides of main roads and comprise clusters of houses with thatched roofs. Work begins and ends with a communal mandi, or bath, and is carried out in the cooler hours of the day to avoid the sun's intense heat.

*T*he market is central to village life and early every morning, villagers make their way there with fruit, vegetables, flowers and handicrafts to sell. The markets are a colourful spectacle. They are usually open-air and bargaining is not uncommon.

# The Cockfight

Village festivals are colourful, more so when cockfights take place. But it is also a gruesome spectacle as roosters, each with a knife attached to one leg, fight to the death. A crowd invariably gathers whenever a cockfight is on. The excitement is palpable as the people in the crowd, sizing up each rooster's chances, place bets on their favourites.

Before the fight starts, the owner of each rooster makes a chant as if instilling in his charge the battle force. Then, on the word "go", uttered by an arbitrator or *pande*, the roosters are released. It is a bloody battle as the two roosters attack each other ferociously, with the knife stabbing at every turn, until one drops dead.

*T*he cockfighting ritual had its origin in black magic as the blood spilled by the defeated rooster was said to appease the spirits of the underworld. Though officially banned, the cockfight is often still staged in villages as a social event for men and as a means to satisfy their betting urge. Roosters are kept in coops (above, left) and lovingly looked after by their owners (above, right).

# Rites of Passage

The various phases of Balinese life, from birth to death, are marked by rituals and ceremonies presided over by priests. Childbirth, childhood, coming of age, marriage, divorce and death have their own special rites.

The root of family life in Bali, as in everywhere else, lies in marriage. Getting married and starting a family is considered one of life's fulfilments for a Balinese. For a man, it signals his entry into the village community as a full-fledged member.

Getting married in Bali is quite different from that in many other societies. When a Balinese couple decides to wed, the man will 'elope' with his girlfriend with the blessings of her parents and stay in a hiding place. The wedding will take place later on an auspicious date. For those from aristocratic backgrounds, the more preferred form of marriage arrangement is to have the parents of a young man approach the father of the girl he fancies for her hand in marriage. Unlike arranged matches elsewhere, the girl has the option to refuse. If she agrees, the young couple are allowed to date and spend time together.

After marriage, the birth of a child is greeted with joy for it signals the beginning of life's cycle. A newborn child is, after all, a reincarnation of an ancestor, thus representing the continuity between the past and present members of a family. Perpetuating the family line is so important that a childless wife can be grounds for a man to divorce her or to take a second wife.

Growing up in Bali is never a lonely experience. The mother attends to the child's needs with grandma and grandpa always ready to help. As soon as the child can walk, he is left to roam freely in the village with other children as company. And although Balinese children do attend school, their education by example and observation is far more precious and useful. Tiny tots, for instance, are exposed to dancing at a tender age, learning by mimicking movements. Bottom, right: Cultural learning begins early in life for the Balinese. Boys, hoping to become dancers, go through their paces with a dancing teacher in a temple in Ubud.

The wedding ceremony of a couple from a noble family. After paying respects to their ancestors at the family shrine and obtaining their blessings, the couple sits on a marriage pavilion before a white-robed priest who blesses the union with incantations in Sanskrit, a sprinkling of holy water, bell ringing and throwing of flowers. A final purification rite is carried out with food, salt and holy water after which the priest marks the forehead of the bride and groom to protect them from evil.

*A*part from eliminating emotional behaviour, the Balinese believe that the filing of the six front teeth into a straight line improves a person's appearance and guards him from evil. Auspicious dates have to be picked for the tooth-filing ceremony; in cases where the cost is considered to be prohibitive, the ceremony can be postponed until just before marriage.

# Tooth-filing

Of all life's rites of passage, perhaps the most significant is the tooth-filing ceremony, which boys and girls at the age of puberty undergo to mark their entry into adulthood.

For the Balinese, sharp canine teeth are for animals only. If these are not eliminated, they will predispose humans to undesirable animalistic behaviour such as lust, anger, greed and drunkenness. Filing is done without anaesthetic. To help reduce pain, holy water is drunk and the ritual is accompanied with much bell-ringing and incantations by priests. The discarded parts of the teeth are then buried next to the ancestral shrine to prevent their use in black magic rituals.

## Death and Cremation

To the Balinese, death is a joyous occasion as it releases the immortal soul from its earthly shape, allowing it to roam freely until it is reincarnated in another form. Practised in Bali as early as the 13th century, cremation completes the cycle of life. However, as it is a costly affair, it does not usually take place immediately after death and a body is buried in a shroud temporarily in the village cemetery after death, to await cremation.

When the day arrives, the body is blessed by the priest who covers it with spices. Symbolic trappings to help him in the next life are placed on various parts of his body. These are steel bits on his teeth for stronger teeth, iron nails on his limbs to give him more strength, pieces of mirror on his eyelids so he can have brighter eyes and jasmine flowers in his nostrils so he can have sweeter breath.

The cremation day's ceremony starts early. At the sounding of the village drums, the remains are carried from the home to the cremation tower. Pallbearers, numbering as many as a hundred, then carry the tower on their shoulders to the cremation grounds in an elaborate procession.

On arrival at the cremation grounds, the sarcophagus is placed on a mound. The relatives give the body a last look before the high priest sprinkles holy water on it, places the effigy and closes the lid. Then the priest sets fire to the mound after a last blessing.

The cremation day's ceremony starts early and is conducted by a high priest. At the sounding of the village drum, the remains are carried from the home to the cremation tower. The whole structure is only lit after it is placed on a mound at the cremation site and after the priest has sprinkled holy water and made his blessings. Following pages: The decorated cremation tower is carried by as many as a hundred pallbearers on their shoulders to the cremation grounds in an elaborate procession. The tower bearers walk in a zig-zag manner deliberately in an attempt to confuse evil spirits and mislead the dead man's spirit so it would not find its way back to the house.

# MYSTICAL BALI

The early inhabitants of Bali, who migrated from peninsular Southeast Asia, were as animistic in their worship as the indigenous Bali Aga people already living on the island. Both shared a common belief that the powerful elements of nature—the sun, sea, wind, mountains and earth—that could wreak havoc in their lives in the form of volcanic explosions, droughts or stormy weather, were inhabited by spirits and thus had to be regularly placated with prayers and offerings.

It is upon this belief in the spirit world that the Hindu religion from Majapahit Java was introduced, resulting in a unique Bali-Hindu religion that combines a mix of spirit worship with Hindu practices. The Balinese, like their Indian counterparts, worship Brahma the Creator, Vishnu the Preserver and Siva the Destroyer as the greatest of the Hindu gods. The Hindu trinity has a Balinese equivalent in the form of the god Mahadewa (or Ida Sang Hyang Widhi Wasa) who resides in Gunung Agung, the holiest and highest of the island's mountains.

Religion and this belief in the underworld play a pivotal role in the life of the Balinese. There are good spirits and evil spirits and there are gods and demons. Because all spirits have magical powers and have the potential to create harm, the Balinese are caught in maintaining the balance between the *kadja* (good forces) and the *kelodi* (evil forces). The duality of these two forces and man being caught in between is symbolised in how the Balinese regard as good versus bad: the mountains as opposed to the sea; day against night; the right side against the left side; life against death.

Much of the daily lives of the Balinese is wrapped up in the performance of rituals, which take many forms: as prayers, the giving of offerings, the performance of sacred dances and rites as well as festival celebrations.

*When a Balinese prays, he can do so privately or within a gathering, usually at a temple, presided over by a priest who then does the praying. Sprinkling water is part of the prayer ceremony: it's a means of 'feeding' the gods the essence of offerings (above). Facing page: A temple decorated elaborately for a festival, with umbrellas, ceremonial offerings and cloths draped over the temple guardians.*

# Offerings

There are different kinds of offerings, from simple ones left on the ground to appease demons to elaborate pieces of art reserved only for the gods. In every village and in the urban areas, in homes, temples, shrines, shops and even on the grounds of resort hotels, the offering ritual is carried out daily.

Even the casual visitor will not fail to notice the shrines at his hotel and how every morning, a young girl or woman, with a tray of offerings and water, will make her rounds. At each of these shrines, she places, in a niche, a beautifully prepared offering made from coconut leaves, with flowers, some rice and an incense stick in the centre. With a flick of her hand, she sprinkles holy water over the offering, so that the deity can partake of the 'essence' of the offering wafted to it by the hand gesture, before moving to the next shrine.

Food offerings may also be placed on the ground or anywhere evil spirits may be lurking, to keep them happy and to thwart any misdoings on their part.

At festival time, the gods are given more elaborate offerings in the form of magnificent arrangements of chicken, fruit, flowers and even money. These are placed on temple altars and after prayers, when the gods have consumed the offerings in essence, these are brought home to be eaten. On days set aside for the placation of evil spirits, on the fifth and 15th day of the month, the offerings can be of anything, even tripe, and these are placed on the ground, to be left behind or eaten by dogs.

The making of offerings is an art, which is learnt mainly by women who create them according to a strict set of rules, taking hours to do so in the case of major festivals.

Prayers are conducted anywhere but most usually where a deity is known to be residing. This could be in a rice field, a mountain, a shrine at home or at a temple. Offerings accompany prayers; the elaborate ones piled high with food, fruit, flowers and even money are for the gods. Prayers are made for harmony, happiness and prosperity in an individual's personal life or for certain favours. When the prayer is granted, even more offerings are made.

*A*t festivals, women walk in colourful processions to temples, with offerings piled high upon their heads. Such processions take place almost every day, with the most elaborate of them occurring during the festival of Kuningan.

77

## Festivals

In Bali, there always seems to be a festival taking place; it could be the birthday of a village temple, New Year's Day, a holy day or the consecration of a new temple. These festivals represent the rites conducted for the propitiation of spirits.

The only way to find out what is happening, and when, is to get hold of a Balinese calendar which maps out the days of divine obligation, the days of celebration and the days determined to be auspicious by the gods for conducting important events, be it the construction of a house or a marriage ceremony. The same goes for *odalan* (temple birthdays), which is celebrated in every village.

*F*estival fever in Bali. Women in a temple procession, dressed in their glittering best (facing page, top). Faithfuls participating in temple celebrations—the religious Kuningan Festival at Mas (facing page, bottom) and at Tanah Lot (left).

79

# Odalan

The *odalan* is one of the main religious festivals celebrated by every village community. Preparations begin days in advance. On such religious occasions, the food is cooked by the men, while the women prepare the offerings at home and bring them in colourful processions into the temple where these are blessed by the *pemangku* (temple guardian).

As the people pray and throw flowers in the direction of the shrines, the *pemangku* blesses them with holy water. He then invites the gods into the temple. The festivities continue all night long with dances, drama performances and music.

*E*very village temple has its odalan which takes place twice a year. It is a celebration that galvanises the entire community. Special odalan offerings are made to be placed at temples and the village is decorated.

81

# Temples

Balinese temples or *pura* are usually deserted except on festival days when they become awash with worshippers and offerings. The *pemangku*, who is dressed in white and belongs to the *sudra* caste, is responsible for the upkeep of the temple. He blesses offerings with holy water prepared by the high priest and organises most of the temple ceremonies. Special religious ceremonies, however, are presided over by the high priest or *pedanda*.

Balinese temples are considered the dwelling places of the gods so when you enter, you find yourself moving from the *kelod* (lowly side) facing the sea towards the *kaja,* which is the mountainside. Many temples are built in terraces so you have to climb upwards to reach the inner area.

Generally, there are two or three enclosed courtyards in a temple, each leading into the other by *candi bentar* (split gates) of carved stone. The courtyards may house the *meru* shrines that are shaped like multi-tiered pagodas, with thatched roofs representing the revered mountains. It is in the innermost courtyard that the most sacred rites are performed in the presence of the gods. Here, too, is found the *padmasana*, a stone shrine with a seat on which the sun god, or Surya, is invited to sit.

*Worshippers gathering for a festival at Besakih, Bali's 'Mother Temple'. Located on the slopes of Gunung Agung, Besakih is the oldest, largest and most sacred of the island's temples.*
*Following pages: Standing in isolated splendour atop a craggy rock outcrop surrounded by swirling waves, is the unique temple of Tanah Lot. At low tide, the sea recedes and worshippers can walk to the temple.*

# Sacred Rites and Dances

As anyone who has ever watched will testify, Bali's sacred dance performances are so intense and powerful, they leave no doubt at all that the performers are possessed. Known as *sanghyang* (deity) dances, these are the rites of ecstasy involving the use of temple mediums who call on certain deities to possess the dancers, helped along by incantations of *cak* and the burning of incense smoke. The power within the dancers enables them to exorcise the village of evil spirits and illnesses.

Among the many *sanghyang* dances is the dance of the angels of worship, or *sanghyang dedari*, performed by two young girls in a trance. Carried on palanquins, the girls are brought to places such as the village crossroads or in front of the home of people who can transform themselves into *leyaks* or witches. The girls are returned to the temple to dance slowly to a choir. As soon as the singing stops, the girls collapse, as the trance is broken. A *pemangku* revives the dancers.

A more vigorous dance is the *sanghyang djaran* in which one or more possessed men prance around on hobbyhorses, dancing over red-hot coals to chase away evil spirits that cause illness in the village.

Equally sacred, though not classified as *sanghyang*, are the *rejang* and *mendet* dances, which are considered part of temple offerings to the gods. These are performed, with slow-paced steps, by women carrying holy water and offerings to give to the gods.

*D*ance is often considered a divine expression and many dances are performed only within the inner courtyard of a temple where the gods are worshipped. Temple dances usually involve the parade of the pusaka (or regalia) kept within the temple (facing page and following pages). Above left: Burning incense smoke is one of the rites of a sanghyang dance. Above right: Women dancing the rejang carry holy water and offerings to the gods.

# ALL OF BALI'S A STAGE

**W**herever you go in Bali, you will often hear the soft lilting melody of a gamelan orchestra, sounding like steady beats on a xylophone, accompanied by what sounds like running water over a pebbled stream. If you listen carefully, you will realise the rhythm is repetitive and catching, nay, mesmerising even. How spellbinding the music can be is more fully appreciated when you attend one of the many theatrical and dance performances that fill a typical day in Bali.

Music is essential to dance performances. Not any kind of music, mind you; rather, each dance calls for a specific type of orchestra. Witness a performance and you will understand why: a dancer melds with the music, becoming at one with it; every tempo a cue to a specific movement.

Ornately costumed and covered with gilded ornaments, the dancer seems mesmerised as he listens and moves in measured steps to the tempo of the music, jerking his head back and forth or side to side, rolling his eyes and gesturing with his hands, in a manner reminiscent of traditional Indian dances. Each gesture conveys a different meaning understood by the audience and every movement, learnt by the dancer since childhood, is determined by tradition; there are no allowances for innovation.

Like the musicians, dancers perform *gratis*, but are well fêted after the show, and if a fee is received, it all goes towards the upkeep of their resplendent costumes. And like their musical counterparts, the dancers belong to a village troupe. But unlike the former who are all males, dancers are of both sexes, beginning their training from the tender age of six, after a selection process that picks out potential performers with the right personality, fitness level and aptitude. The young dancers come under the wing of a former accomplished dancer.

*T*wo young boys performing the gopala folk dance in Batuan. Every facial expression and movement of the hands and feet convey a meaning in this dance of the cowherd (facing page). The baris dancer (above), depicting a warrior, is even more expressive, darting his eyes, flickering his fingers and prancing on his feet.

In Bali, there is rarely a dance without music and the gamelan orchestra (above) is central to any performance. Facing page : The kebyar trompong dance is a demanding performance as the performer has to be both a dancer and a musician.

# The Orchestra

Whether it is an entertaining shadow play, a mime, a dance drama, a festival, a feast or a sombre religious ritual, no performance takes place without the music provided by a gamelan orchestra. The size of the orchestra and types of instruments used depends on the occasion, but generally, these are percussive in nature, comprising gongs, xylophones and drums.

The basic gamelan orchestra is made up of a series of xylophone-like instruments known as *gangsa*. These are bronze metal strips sitting atop beautifully carved wooden frames. A musician sits cross-legged behind the *gangsa* and hits the strips with a wooden mallet to produce the notes. The *gangsa* comes in various sizes, depending on the notes required, and is usually played with one hand; in the case of the *gender*, which has ten notes, two hands are used. Bamboo flutes, which produce those lilting melodies, and cymbals, sometimes accompany the *gangsa*.

Gongs are also present. Made of brass, each gong, suspended from a carved wooden frame, is hit with a mallet to produce deep resounding notes. Lighter melodies may be provided by the *trompong* and *reyong*, which are horizontally suspended sets of 10 and 13 bronze bulb-shaped bells respectively, that are struck by several musicians using wooden rods. Then, there are the drums or *kendang*, which come in pairs. Double-ended with a diaphragm covering each side, these drums, beaten with the palms of hands and fingers, provide the rhythm of the music.

94

*M*embers of a gamelan orchestra (facing page). The Ramayana Ballet performance (above) is one of Bali's most classic dances.

The gamelan orchestra comprises different types of instruments, including double-ended drums known as kendang, bronze gongs and xylophone-like instruments struck with wooden mallets.

## Types of Dances

If music is the food of love, dance is what nurtures the soul. In Bali, this is particularly true as dancing here is not only for one's own pleasure and the enjoyment of others, it is also a form of communion with the gods.

Balinese dance forms are very different and all very dazzling but they can be categorised generally under secular or sacred dances. The sacred dances are reserved for mystical rites and many of the performers are actually in a trance when they are on stage. They are held in the inner courtyard of temples; some better known dances are the *rejang*, the *baris gede*, the *mendet*, the *barong* and the *djanger*.

The secular dances are what most tourists are familiar with. They are classical and modern dances, performed in the outer courtyard. Among them are the popular *legong*, *oleg tambulilingan*, *kebyar*, *baris*, *arja* and *sendratari*. The best known dance among tourists, as it is easily witnessed on many beach resorts, is the spectacular *kecak* or monkey dance, which has its origins in the mystical realm. Indeed, though considered a secular dance, watching the dancers caught up in a frenzy as they chant "cak, cak, cak", it is difficult not to think that they have been transported into the world of the spiritual.

*The mask of the barong with bulging eyes and long teeth (below and facing page) may look frightening but this entertaining dance expresses best the eternal Balinese struggle between good and evil forces. The barong is the village protector, fighting against the evil forces of the rangda, queen of witches.*

*T*he kecak or 'monkey dance' is the best known among tourists (following pages). It is performed by a cast of up to a hundred bare-chested men, dressed only in sarongs. Sitting in concentric circles, they chant "cak, cak, cak" in unison as accompaniment to the unfolding drama, based on a Ramayana epic.

# The Legong

This is the most classical of all Balinese dances, performed only by girls and always in a pair. It is a traditional dance with precise steps and movements of the head, shoulders, body and eyes, without even a hint of a smile on the face. All expressions, however, are captured in the eyes, which dart this way and that, and sometimes do a roll. There are 18 attitudes adopted by the dancers who move in tandem with one another. Very often, the *legong* depicts an episode from the mythical *Malat*. This tells the story of a prince, Lasem, and a princess, Rangkesari, represented by the two girls. Prince Lasem has kidnapped the princess who is engaged to marry another, the Crown Prince of Kahuripan. The princess pleads to be set free. Prince Lasem refuses and sets forth instead to confront the crown prince. En route, he encounters a raven, a bird of ill-omen; when he meets the crown prince, a fight ensues and Lasem is killed.

The story is unfolded in dance sequences accompanying the narration by a storyteller.

*E*xquisitely costumed legong dancers (above and facing page). The legong is another Balinese classical dance tradition and depicts a story from the Malat, the Balinese version of 'A Thousand and One Nights'.

# Drama and Theatre

Balinese drama, today, is derived from the folk theatre of the *wayang kulit* which was a travelling theatre, much like the western Punch and Judy version. Enduring and entertaining—that is the secret of the *wayang kulit* performance where the actors are leather stick-puppets adroitly manipulated by a *dalang* (master puppeteer) behind a white cotton screen lit up by an oil lamp. The *dalang* also narrates the story that unfolds, taken from the *Ramayana* classics, often injecting his own dialogue in the process. The *dalang* performs his traditional version of the Balinese theatre, from village to village, carrying the tools of his trade in a box.

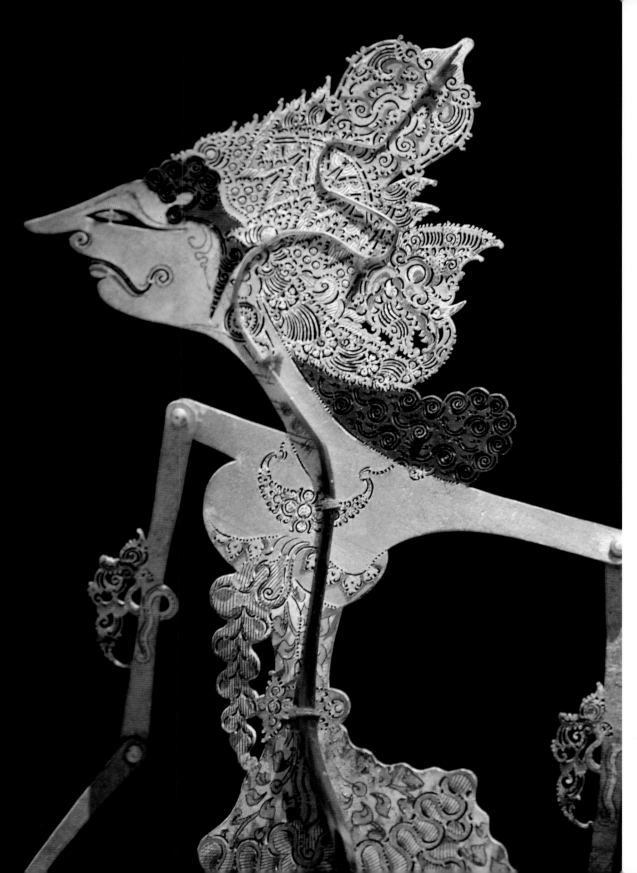

Against a flickering oil lamp, a dalang or shadow puppet master manipulates his handcrafted leather stick-puppets to dramatise a story from the Ramayana epic (facing page, bottom). This theatrical performance, known as wayang kulit or shadow puppet theatre, was the basic form of Balinese entertainment. The dalang often makes and paints his own puppets and even carries them in a wooden box, travelling from village to village, staging his itinerant show. The puppets have moveable arms, which allow for easy manipulation.

*The* most entertaining of all Balinese dance forms is the topeng (right), which uses the mask to define characters which can be an effeminate young man, a passionate lover, a doddering old man or a haughty aristocrat.
Facing page: A gambuh actor (top) and performers in a dance drama (bottom).
Following pages: Another theatrical art form by telek dancers in Peliatan; the white-masked dancers represent the good forces.

From *wayang kulit* came the mask dances so beloved of the modern Balinese stage today. Perhaps the most entertaining and humorous of all Balinese dance forms is the *topeng* which uses the mask to define characters which can be an effeminate young man, a passionate lover, a doddering old man or haughty aristocrat. The drama that unfolds usually has a moral to tell despite the buffooning that takes place. It relates to Balinese history or current events, which like all Balinese dramas, has the good guys reigning supreme over the bad.

Quite often, the mask dramas also re-enact classical epics from Javanese history such as the *Ramayana and Mahabharata*.

# ART AND LIFE INTERTWINED

For the Balinese, art is part and parcel of life, unlike in many other societies where it is often associated only with the elite. However many times you may have visited the island, you will still be astonished at the high quality of art you can find in even the tiniest studio in a back alley of a village in Bali's highlands and the variety of new, quality handicrafts that are produced every year.

*F*or the Balinese, art and life mirror each other. The Kamasan paintings with their wayang-style figures which decorate the ceiling of the Kerta Gosa or Hall of Justice (facing page), and the sculpture at the same place in Klungkung (above), were created for the gods.

The Balinese are a naturally talented and creative people, with a strong artistic tradition. It all began long before the arrival of tourism. The first form of arts and crafts that evolved was for the benefit of the gods alone. The stone statues carved by Balinese craftsmen and the first paintings they produced were religiously inspired—to decorate temple gates, compounds and palaces.

At a time when public education was yet to be available, these arts and crafts also had an educational role to play. People, then and now, learnt by emulating others before them; there was no need for in-born talent. This matter-of-fact approach is witnessed every day in villages. Even today, you will see children, as young as six years old, who are given a few hours' coaching daily in artists' studios where they learn to draw, by copying someone else's painting first, and then honing their skills, with guidance from a teacher.

It was the Europeans who first recognised the economic potential of the magnificent handiwork of the Balinese. From the initial wave that arrived in the early 1900s to the present day, they have helped the Balinese to exploit their traditional skills by encouraging them to produce objects of practical use and in a design that would appeal to the tourist. Thus from carving stone and painting religious scenes for themselves and for the gods, the Balinese went on to carving wood and painting landscapes to earn a living, when they realised there was a market for their artistic work.

# Arts and Crafts

Most of Bali's woodcarvings can be found in Mas where not only statues and masks are carved, but also furniture and objets d'art. In the neighbouring centre of Ubud, there are art studios and galleries galore where you can watch local artists painstakingly at work, painting on canvas, scenes of nature and everyday life in Bali. At Celuk, silver and gold jewellery ateliers can be found in abundance. In Bona, you can find mats, baskets, lanterns and screens made out of bamboo or woven from the palmyra palm-leaf. Coiled baskets are available in the Pengosekan area near Ubud and stone carvings in Batubulan.

These days, the stone carvings have transcended religious purposes and you can find figurines such as Balinese mythical figures, whimsical designs like frogs and grotesque folk figures, playing different types of musical instruments, to grace any home garden. Balinese pottery is also a good buy. Then there are the colourful and highly decorative furniture pieces such as chests of drawers, stools and mini-cabinets; cast-iron objects such as wine racks and candleholders, plus coloured glassware, soapstone carvings and elegant stationery from recycled paper.

Many Balinese arts and crafts today are still made using traditional methods, and with the aim of achieving both aesthetic and practical value. For instance, the traditional double-*ikat* or *kamben geringsing* textile, which tourists buy to make wall hangings, continues to be woven in the Bali Aga village of Tenganan in East Bali. Other traditional arts and crafts include hand-woven baskets and mats, which can grace any modern home, and the *lontar*, which are paintings of *Ramayana* legends on miniature accordion-like palm-leaf strips.

*Bali's sacred textile, the double-ikat geringsing (below), is hand-woven by the Bali Aga people and still survives to this day.*
*Facing page: Chiselling out of stone or carving out of wood, Balinese artisans are true masters of their art.*

*D*ecorative wooden carvings and masks in Ubud (facing page, top left and bottom); an artisan at work in the Bali Aga village of Tenganan (top right). Traditional clay figurines are popular among tourists who bring them home to grace their gardens (bottom right). Above: A decorated courtyard in Ubud.

## Architecture and Sculpture

The most detailed form of art can perhaps be seen in Bali's temple architecture. Every visitor is acquainted with the split gate or *candi bentar,* the entrance gate that leads into the outer courtyard of a temple. Split because it represents two halves of a mountain, a symbol of holiness, and symbolising the splitting of the universe, the gates are ornately carved with figures representing the gods and temple guardians, monsters, animals, flowers and other motifs. The second gateway, the *padu raksa*, leading into the inner courtyard, is even more ornately carved. In this courtyard are several shrines; some consist of a simple platform with a thatched roof, others are mounted with a series of roofs in diminishing sizes.

All Balinese temples are distinct from one another but they are built according to established rules. They all have the stamp of their architect who uses his own body to measure the heights and distances of the gateways and buildings within the temple to plan the layout. The height of the main gateway, for instance, is determined by the length of the architect's hands.

Just as ornately decorated as its temples are the opulent palaces of Bali's former kings, known as *puri*. The doorway to a palace is usually intricately carved with religious and mythical figures. One such figure often seen on palace gateways is the *karang ceweri*, a monstrous being with bulging eyes, long teeth and fingernails and a hanging tongue.

*B*alinese temples are constructed in a series of terraced courts and stairways, culminating in the pyramidal meru (pagoda-like roof) made usually of black thatch (left). Stone statues of deities guard the entrances while carvings of masks, monsters and other motifs decorate the walls and sides (bottom left and right). Facing page: Like in other Balinese temples, the inner courtyard of the Tirta Empul Temple in Tampaksiring is a sanctuary for the gods.

The Puri Lukisan Museum in Ubud (right) is an example of modern Balinese architecture while the floating pavilion of the Hall of Justice in Klungkung (facing page) is a traditional form.
Below: Stone carvings such as these can be found in Balinese temples and other architectural structures.

# Painting

The early paintings of the Balinese were of religious scenes in a narrative sequence, unfolding stories with moral themes, picture by picture, similar to a comic strip. These were traditional tales painted according to set rules and in a flat style. They depicted legends of deities, demons, mythological creatures, royalty and the common folk, always with the good triumphing over the bad. The characteristically earthy and muted colours were derived from natural materials such as barks and leaves. The best examples of these are the frescoes at the Hall of Justice in Klungkung and the palm-leaf accordion-like books of the indigenous Bali Aga, depicting episodes from the *Ramayana*.

Then, in the early 1900s, Western artists came and introduced their art forms to the Balinese who, adaptable as always, blended it with their own. The result: a modern Balinese art that broke free from traditional formulae, giving rein instead to individual imagination and the use of vibrant colours. The Balinese artist also learnt to apply the three-dimensional concept.

Among the more influential of the Western artists were Walter Spies, a German who settled in Ubud in 1927, and Dutch artist Rudolf Bonnet who arrived in 1929, also choosing to stay in Ubud. Their long-lasting legacy is the Pita Maha (Great Shining) Painters' Cooperative that they founded in 1934 with the then Prince of Ubud, to promote and enhance the talents of local artists.

Thanks to this association, which has organised exhibitions in Java and Europe, many Balinese artists have received international exposure and recognition for their talents. Without a doubt, their works abroad have captured, and will continue to capture, the imagination of many and inspire them to see Bali for themselves.

*Balinese paintings are characteristically detailed, and in the early days, featured astrological calendars (with each square of the months painted with a scene), mythical motifs (left) and moralistic themes such as this painting of Hell on the ceiling of the Kerta Gosa (bottom). From using basic colours, painters moved on to using brighter colours and other media such as oils on canvasses. Daily scenes are still a favourite subject.*

*Facing page: A painter at work, while an artisan chisels on lontar to create palm-leaf books.*

*U*bud has a thriving artists' community as these paintings can testify (left and facing page). Art galleries and studios can be found even in the tiniest villages.

Another of Bali's famous expatriate artists was Spanish painter, Antonio Blanco, whose whimsical works, so reminiscent of his compatriot Salvador Dali, with whom he identified, can be viewed in his house which has been converted into the newly opened Blanco Renaissance Museum in Ubud. His highly sensual works, which focused on women, celebrated the Balinese dancer (represented by his wife Ni Ronji, who was his muse) as an art form. Some 300 works, including lithographs and paintings are on display.

*A sample of Blanco's celebrated art form: A Balinese dancer, depicted by his wife in her younger days (above, right).*

*F*acing page: An unfinished canvas, an array of oil paints and quirky works of art remain untouched in Antonio's Blanco's studio. Blanco had a style of his own which he pursued in his well-preserved studio, which is surrounded by greenery and tranquillity, in the heart of Ubud. He would paint, sitting cross-legged on the floor. In later years, as he became stiffer in his joints, and could no longer sit cross-legged, the floor was carved out to accommodate a platform where he would sit, tucking his legs into a cavity below.

*A*bove, left: The Blanco family temple within the grounds of the museum. Above, right: An appropriately Dali-esque sculpture marks the entrance (previous page) to the Blanco Renaissance Museum. Facing page: This sign says it all, beckoning visitors to catch a glimpse of the extraordinary life of Antonio Blanco.

*B*athed in the soft glow of light, this candi bentar (split gate), which marks the entrance to a temple, beckons visitors to enter.

# Bali

## THROUGH PAINTINGS

*A relic of an old painting at Batur temple, Kintamani. From the earliest times, the Balinese had a fine eye for artistic detail and often illustrated scenes from the Ramayana and Mahabharata epics.*

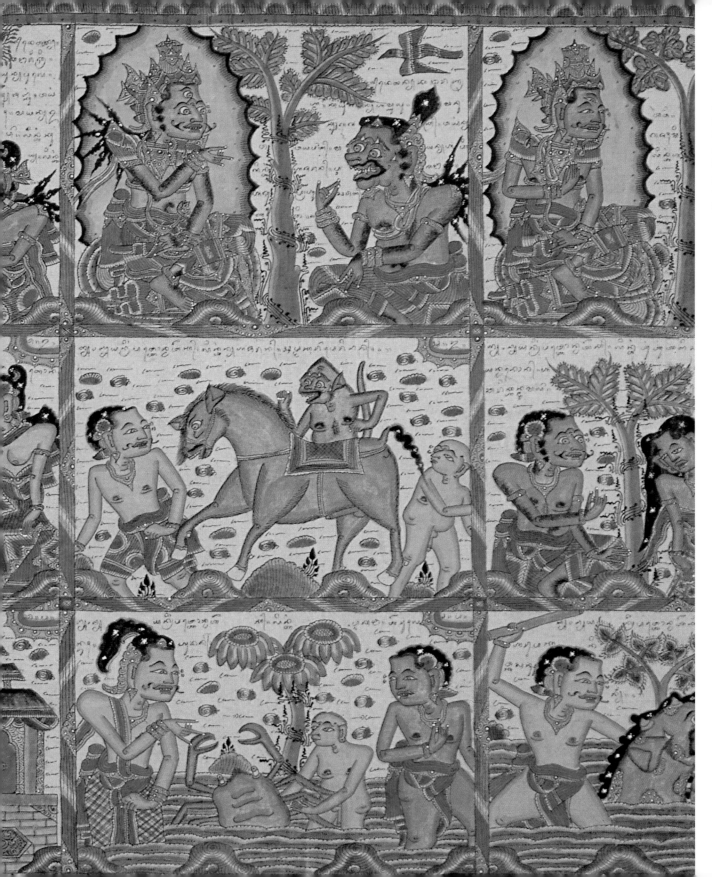

**A** traditional Balinese calendar or tika. Each month features 35 days and each day is represented by a square which is filled with a painted scene illustrating the eternal struggle between good and evil.

131

*E*xamples of traditional Kamasan paintings (above and facing page), named after its origin in the village of Kamasan in the former kingdom of Gelgel. The paintings were an ancient version of the comic strip and they were done in a series, unfolding a story. Mythical figures, gods, demons, monsters and the nobility were featured, painted in a puppet-like form.

Some of the best examples of Kamasan-style paintings can be viewed in the Puri Lukisan Museum in Ubud. Typical themes include the need to uphold morality by depicting the Balinese version of hell (far left), and battles fought by the gods against monsters, in this case, the god of the sea against demons of the underwater world (left).

*Traditional scenes of rice fields with farmers engaging in various agricultural activities are a popular theme of many Balinese artists.*

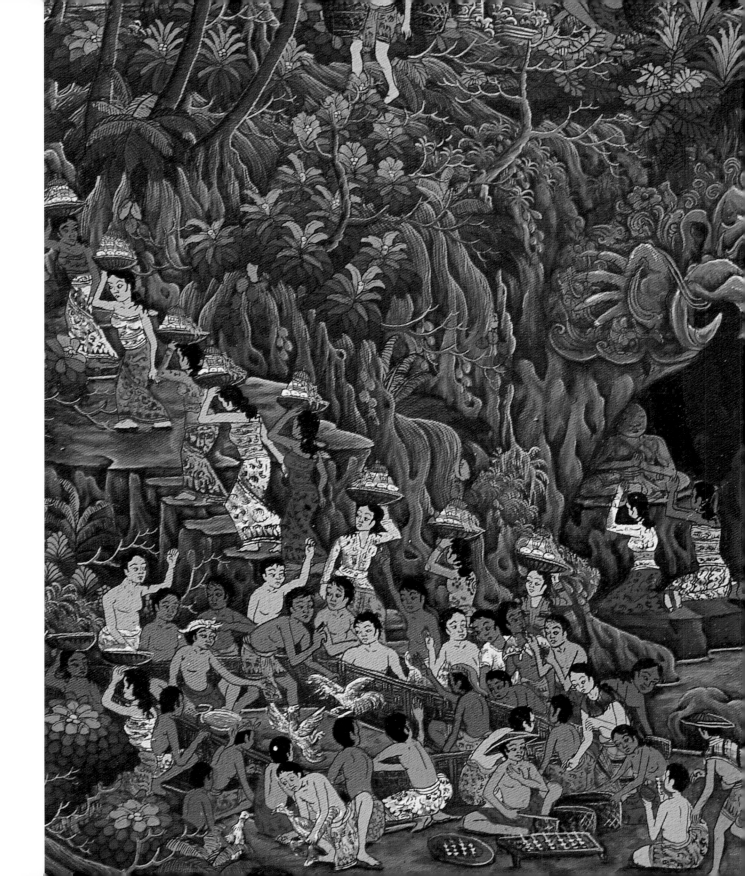

German artist Walter Spies, who came to Bali in 1925, exerted a profound influence on the local artistic scene when he introduced a surrealistic style of painting. It is an influence that is reflected in this comtemporary painting by I Wayan Kaler.

139

NI NYOMAN DAH NI KETUT
BALI 1976
R. BONNET

"SULING PLAYER"
BALI 1976
R·BONNET

*R*udolf Bonnet (1895-1978) was a Dutch artist who was among the earliest European painters to arrive in Bali and to teach the Balinese classical art techniques. La Fille Nyoman et Ketut (The Woman Nyoman and Ketut, *facing page) and* Le Joueur de Flute *(The Flautist,* left) were painted by the artist in 1976.

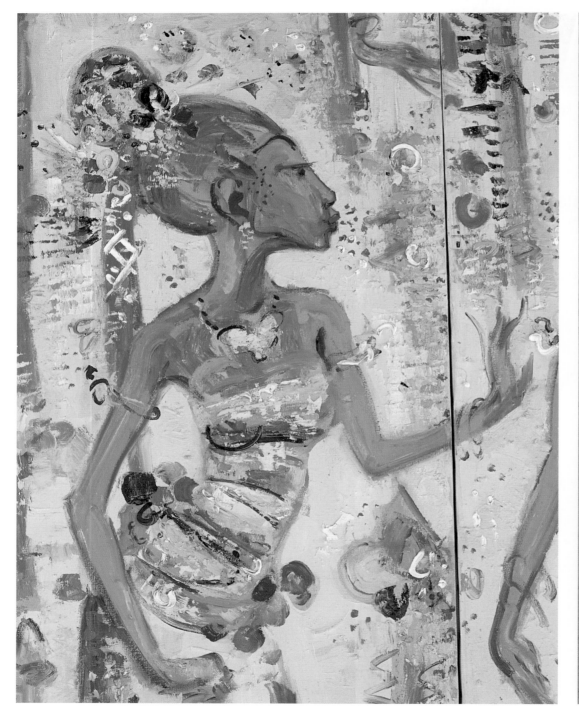

142

*A modern painting by Nyoman Gunarsa (far left), who employs both figurative and abstract styles in his work. Many of his figures, such as this, are not done in strong graphic lines but by the juxtaposition of delicate hues. Several of his works include characters from classical tales and traditional dance. Left: Traditional Balinese painting of a market scene by Garjita Sobrat.*

A *painting of Gunung Batur by Affandi in 1986. The grand old man of Indonesian painting, Affandi's works are characterised by his thick impasto technique, such as in this painting, which shows strong movement and expressive tension.*